# IMPROVING RISK COMMUNICATION

## WORKING PAPERS

Prepared for:
Committee on Risk Perception and Communication

Commission on Physical Sciences, Mathematics, and Resources
Commission on Behavioral and Social Sciences and Education

National Research Council

NATIONAL ACADEMY PRESS
Washington, D.C. 1989

## PREFACE

This volume contains papers that were originally prepared for the use of the National Research Council's Committee on Risk Perception and Communication. The Committee commissioned these two case studies as part of its study on the process of risk communication, the content of risk messages, and ways to improve risk communication.

The working papers do not necessarily reflect the judgment or position of the committee or the National Research Council. They have not been subjected to the internal review procedures that apply to reports prepared by NRC committees. Responsibility for the case studies rests with the authors.

The two case studies were intended as examples of situations involving risk communication. They are not intended to present independent positions or interpretations on the subject of risk communication.

Lawrence E. McCray
Study Director

# TABLE OF CONTENTS

A CASE STUDY OF THE 1980/82 MEDFLY CONTROVERSY IN CALIFORNIA    1
    Emery M. Roe

COMMUNICATING CORPORATE DISASTER    29
    The Aldicarb Oxime Release at the Union Carbide Plant
    at Institute, West Virginia on August 11, 1985
        Rob Coppock

# A Case Study of the 1980/82 Medfly Controversy in California.

Emery M. Roe
Graduate School of Public Policy
University of California, Berkeley

```
I like to compare the Medfly Project to Christopher Columbus's first voyage.
Columbus didn't know where he was going, didn't know where he was when he got
there, and didn't know where he had been when he got back.  But Columbus had
it easy.  At least he was alone.  If Columbus had sailed under the same
constraints we endured in fighting the medfly, his ship would have been
purchased from the lowest bidder by the Department of General Services, and
his crew would have been hired for him by the State Personnel Board.  The
rigging on the ship would have been arranged by State and Federal Occupational
and Health Safety regulators, not for sailing, but for crew safety.  And on
the poop deck, he would have had a technical advisory committee of renowned
geographers giving him up-to-the-minute input on direction and risk/benefit.
To top it off, he would have had a full complement of television, press and
radio newsmen running around on deck recording for the folks back home in
Spain every time a crewman slipped on deck or grumbled about the food, his
opinion of Columbus, the voyage and so on...Columbus had it easy.
```

From remarks by the state co-manager of the 1980/82 California Medfly Project[1]

## Introduction.

This paper provides a case study of state/federal risk communication along multiple dimensions. The infestation and spread of Mediterranean fruit flies ("medflies") in California during the first years of the 1980s posed what was perceived to be a major economic threat to the state's agriculture, while at the same time leading to intergovernmental eradication efforts that were taken to entail substantial health, environmental, political, bureaucratic and professional risks as well. Although it is not unusual to cast complex public policy problems in terms of multiple risks, what makes the 1980/82 California medfly controversy of particular interest is its detailed documentation. This case study draws on the recollections of a number of the key participants in the controversy, recorded at a seminar series sponsored by the Survey Research Center, University of California, Berkeley. Unless otherwise stated, all figures and quotes below are from a draft volume of the edited transcripts and chapters based on these recollections[2].

Sometimes candid, sometimes self-serving, sometimes post hoc rationalizations, the accounts of the controversy's major actors do not make for a straightforward history of what "actually" happened during the crisis. Interpretations of what took place at key meetings, not surprisingly, vary greatly. For the purposes of this paper, though, the many different perspectives of the controversy's important actors have one great virtue: The extensive quotes and paraphrases recorded below allow us to detail and contrast the wide range and variability in how risks associated with an important public policy issue are frequently perceived and how these perceptions are often communicated and responded to.

**Background.**

In June 1980 several medflies were found in two widely separated counties of California, Los Angeles and Santa Clara. A Medfly Project was immediately created in the California Department of Food and Agriculture (CDFA) to deal with the outbreak. The following month a technical review committee, later known as the Technical Advisory Committee (TAC) and consisting largely of professional entomologists, was established to advise the Project and the public on eradication efforts. A ground program was initiated eventually consisting of fruit-tree stripping, localized application of pesticides, and the release of sterile medflies (known as the Sterile Insect Technique [SIT] whereby young male medflies are sterilized through irradiation, released as adults, and mate with wild female flies to produce nonviable eggs).

The ground program was applied to 489 square miles of LA County, and eradication there was declared by mid-December, 1980. However, the Santa Clara infestation had continued to grow throughout the county and into adjacent county areas, spreading from some 150 square miles at the end of September 1980 to over 200 square miles by the end of November that year. By late 1980, officials in the United States Department of Agriculture (USDA) were maintaining that aerial spraying with a malathion bait mixture was necessary to eradicate this infestation, which was probably more extensive than official estimates indicated. The aerial spraying proposal, though, encountered strong opposition from environmental groups, politicians, scientists and academics (including members of the TAC) such that CDFA eventually agreed to postpone action. Citizen and local government opposition to aerial spraying was particularly vocal within Santa Clara

County at this time, e.g, local physicians and pharmacology faculty at Stanford University came out against spraying while city councils passed resolutions seeking to prohibit such spraying over their jurisdictions. A formal risk assessment undertaken at this time by the state's Department of Health Services (DHS) concluded, however, that the chances of such spraying causing cancer in an exposed infant were in the region of one-in-a-million.

The ground program appeared to be effective throughout the winter, but June 1981 saw a fresh outbreak of medflies in Santa Clara County. On July 8, Governor Brown made the politically controversial announcement that the ground spraying program would be greatly expanded in order to deal with the re-emergence. The US Secretary of Agriculture responded by threatening to quarantine the state's fruit exports if aerial spraying was not begun immediately. On July 10 Brown gave the order to begin spraying malathion by air. Some state and international quarantines on California fruit were imposed, but eventually lifted. In September 1982, CDFA and USDA held a joint conference to declare that medfly eradication had been achieved in California. For ease of reference, a summary of these events has been provided in the Appendix's short chronology.

Over $100 million was spent by federal and state authorities to eradicate the medfly during this period. Another $40 million was estimated to have been lost by state growers when other countries and states rejected California fruit. More than 1,300 square miles a week were sprayed malathion by air, while several deaths resulted from accidents attributed to the aerial spraying program as a whole[3].

## The Main Actors, Institutions, and Risk Dimensions Of The Medfly Controversy.

The basic feature of the medfly controversy was that there were no widely accepted or clear-cut technical and scientific reasons to be in favor or against the ground-based program, the aerial spraying program, or some combination thereof[4]. As the Medfly Project's state co-manager put it,

In the medfly public policy debate, the...technical information available to both the public and project management was constantly changing throughout the life of the project, and it was difficult or impossible for advisors and managers to accurately assess the risks and benefits associated with various technical components of the program...[Nor was the public] able to evaluate the severity of the problem or assess the degree of risk associated with the various solutions[5].

Obviously, the costs and benefits associated with the two basic eradication alternatives of ground and aerial spraying would have been assessed in any case from a number of different, at times conflicting, perspectives--political, economic, organizational and professional, among others. Yet the numerous unknowns of a technical and scientific nature made such a composite assessment one of the few certainties the controversy had. Adding to the pervasive sense of technical uncertainty was the fact that much of the politics, bureaucracy, and science of the medfly eradication program was changing over time and with them the risk perceptions associated with that program's various remedies. Not only was the controversy's cast of characters and relations a long one, including state and federal politicians, science advisors, environmental groups, departmental and interdepartmental rivalries, the interests of agribusiness, and by no means last, the media and the public. Also, their variety and numbers ensured that the controversy turned out to be several different controversies perceived to have several different risks that were not just economic, health and environmental in nature, but political, professional, and organizational as well as shall be seen momentarily.

In sum, multiple risk perceptions were associated with both the medfly infestation and its eradication efforts. Such risks, in turn, were realized and communicated in several specific, ultimately overlapping, ways--namely, scientific and technical uncertainties of medfly monitoring, organizational and group conflict, politics, the role of the media in the controversy, and the public's reaction to the various alternatives--which are discussed below. This case study concludes with a discussion about the way in which, in spite of all these differences and disagreements, the Medfly Project was a success.

## Managing The Uncertain Science of Medfly Detection and Eradication.

From the outset, a major and continuing source of contention among the controversy's major players centered around the difficulties in interpreting just what the medflies caught in specially-constructed detection traps really signified. While the trap finds confirmed the presence of the adult medfly, they did not indicate the depth of the infestation, particularly for medfly larvae (in fruit) or pupae (in the ground). But the problems of interpretation went much further and were more pervasive, especially in the areas of medfly detection, sampling, and the management of both.

In the opinion of one informed source, the local officials who had not treated the original medfly finds as a matter of priority "didn't know the true meaning" of the flies they had trapped[6]. So too for CDFA's initially slow response to these finds, at least according to its principal staff entomologist: "We didn't realize the significance of those two flies combined with that low a trap density in Santa Clara...so we didn't take the action we should have"[7]. Trap records remained incomplete and not summarized in a fashion that the Project could usefully utilize, noted one of the USDA's leading entomologists[8]. Some traps even appear to have been sabotaged[9]. Perhaps even more troublesome was the fact that Project technicians were unable to distinguish trapped sterile and wild medflies from each other. Furthermore, why only female flies continued to be caught in the traps that relied entirely on male attractants was never fully explained. A different type of trap had to be introduced because the original type "loaded up like a piece of fly paper" with steriles after their release[10]. More disturbing was the fact that no one was able to decide whether the trap finds at the outset of the mid-1981 re-emergence of medflies were in reality due to (1) the release of "steriles" left fertile because of improper irradiation, (2) the survival of medflies over winter, which earlier research said was not possible under Santa Clara conditions, (3) the Project's defective medfly monitoring and detection procedures, or (4) a combination of these factors and others[11]. Finally, the eventual absence of any trap finds by September 1982, when eradication had been declared for the final infested area, could be explained, according to one well-known university entomologist, by several scenarios other than one claiming eradication had been achieved through aerial spraying with malathion[12]. That widespread malathion spraying and the disappearance of infestations have been frequently correlated in the past was just that, a correlation and not proof of effectiveness, according to this scientist.

The key participants in the controversy responded differently to this basic informational uncertainty. Some tried to find ways to reduce it and thereby better estimate risks, others only succeeded in increasing the uncertainty, while a few took the uncertainty as prima facie evidence of unacceptably high levels of risk associated with one or the other eradication alternative.

Earlier on, the Medfly Project management and the TAC, eventually the major proponents of aerial spraying, had come to a consensus over what kind of trap finds would be taken as reflecting a medfly outbreak sufficiently severe to warrant aerial spraying with malathion[13]. The criteria agreed upon were recognized by these people to be somewhat arbritary, but necessary. In addition, while the Project managers were often at a loss over how to interpret the trap information, they did have a computer model that told the story of the medfly's life cycle in several useful ways for them (in particular, it explained how the medflies could overwinter, contrary to previous research findings). As the Project's federal co-manager put it: "...one thing that really gave our program credibility towards the end...[was the] computer model for calculating the medfly life cycles under San Jose climatic conditions. It was a godsend to us and made what we said acceptable to the Japanese, the Floridians, and to whoever else [wanted to quarantine Californian fruit]"[14]. Finally, after great resistance by some of its parties, a protocol specifying how the aerial spraying of malathion was to proceed had been hammered out and agreed upon in July 1981, a protocol that kept the Project on track and "was our bible", according to the Project's federal co-manager[15]. In short, the outbreak criteria, computer model, and protocol allowed a number of the key participants who were not averse to spraying with malathion to take action as if they knew whether or not the empirical merits of situation warranted that spraying.

Those who were averse to aerial spraying and in favor of the ground program had a much more difficult time in reducing informational uncertainties and assessing medfly-related risks. The major component of the ground program--the release of sterile flies--had many methodological problems that lessened the ability of its proponents to interpret basic information provided by the trap finds. One was the already-mentioned difficulty in distinquishing steriles from wild medflies; others, even more intractable, were evident. Correctly reading the meaning of results obtained from different or unrecorded trap densities was not the only sampling problem. The head of the Project's Quality Control unit complained about the unreality of meeting acceptable sampling standards. When a professional statistician indicated that a 10% sample of each sterile fly container was required, she pointed out that,

on the average, we received 68 million flies a day. It would take one technician 262 years or 94,586 technicians working twenty-four hours to sample ten percent of a mixed population. That is impossible...A decision was never reached about sample size, so I used my judgment[16].

On the face of it, the "arbitrariness" of her decision was no different from that of the outbreak criteria, computer model, or protocol mentioned in the preceding paragraph, save in one crucially important respect. The Project's sampling techniques provided trap information in a form that was of more use to the supporters of aerial spraying that it was to the supporters of SIT. Bait spray programs, such as that of aerially spraying of malathion, rely on discrete data that are demonstrably measurable, while sterile fly release programs are based on continuously variable data, having probability limits that are much less well-defined. One entomologist member of the TAC explained the difficulty and difference this way,

The high quality of data for bait sprays lies in their discrete testable elements. The toxicant, the bait, the dosage, and the formulation are all testable individually...Ultimately, our "comfortableness" with the data derived from the bait spray experiments comes from the fact that it is quantal, based on dead flies with yes or no data. Thereby you get yes or no advice....The [sterile insect technique] data are, by nature, variable and incomplete, and they don't give yes-no answers. Decisions about sterile flies always involve trade-offs...[17]

The supporters of the ground program also had problems in making a clear-cut case against aerial spraying. Opposition to aerial spraying with malathion was fueled by media reports of the very real dissent within the Department of Health Services over the methodology used and conclusions drawn in its risk analysis of this alternative. The assessment was based on the "worst case scenario" thought possible under aerial spraying and eventually concluded that, probabilistically, there was a one-in-a-million chance of an exposed infant contracting cancer from the aerial spraying of malathion. Yet, even though malathion is one of the few pesticides whose effects on humans has received detailed research, one of the DHS officials who undertook the assessment concluded that the department's risk assessment methodology had important limitations. He complained that "[t]here is no consensus on a methodology for [treating]...events where the initial event may have been improbable, but it sets up greater probabilities for secondary errors"[18]. The departmental disagreement over how to compute acute and chronic health risks associated with malathion centered around "the tail end of the probability curve" and "the possibility of relatively remote, very low probability events, which in some cases required concurrently occurring events in order to produce a situation where a small number of individuals would be adversely affected"[19].

The effect of such internal dissent when publicized worked in opposing directions. Supporters of aerial spraying pointed out that these methodological concerns did not disprove the DHS report's basic conclusion about the relatively low risk associated with malathion spraying (added to which, the supporters of the ground program seem not to have undertaken their own risk assessment of the chemicals used in that program, some of which--particularly diazinon and fenthion--were potentially far more hazardous that malathion). Critics of the aerial spraying, however, claimed that such dissent, when combined with other criticisms leveled against the DHS report (e.g., it was charged that the report underestimated the number of sprayings, did not take into account uneven dosages or extraordinary sensitivity of some people to malathion, and did not properly question National Cancer Institute data used in their analysis[20]), was itself a sufficiently good indication of the high uncertainty and risks associated with malathion spraying by air.

## Organizational and Group Conflict.

Intradepartmental differences over how to assess the risks associated with the proposed solutions to the medfly infestation were complemented and in some cases accentuated by equally real differences, both within the same profession or interest group as well as between different agencies, bureaucracies and interest groups, over matters relevant to the more general assessment of associated risks. How you stand depends on where you sit, and this was nowhere more true than in the medfly controversy.

*Intergroup Conflict.* Agribusiness and environmental groups were at odds with each other in this controversy as they frequently are on other issues. Contrary to the views of the fruit growers, environmentalists often argued that the effort should be one of controlling the medfly, not eradicating it: "...it might be far cheaper to learn how to develop a mix of strategies to control [the medfly] below an economic threshold...Once you learn how to live with it you may decide that it's not a bad thing after all. The world had to live with it; and, by the way, most of the world is living with the medfly"[21]. The representative of one of the more important environmental interest groups in the controversy claimed: "People...were saying that medfly was going to destroy California's agricultural industry--billions and billions of dollars down the tubes. But medfly can't destroy our entire agricultural industry. Only a small proportion of the industry would be susceptible..."[22]. However, the estimated $40 million--and it is only an estimate--lost to fruit growers because of quarantines does indicate agribusiness had some incentive to ensure that eradication, rather than control, took place, given eradication was the requirement other states and countries imposed on their importation of California fruit.

*Interdepartmental Conflict.* Departmental battles over turf colored the perceptions of risk associated with the two principal eradication alternatives of ground or aerial spraying. Such conflicts can be found throughout the history of the "co-management" of the Medfly Project, where

USDA and CDFA were each to assign a co-manager to the Project, both of whom in turn were expected to work in close consultation and cooperation with various county officials. The conflicts arising from this arrangement were probably no different than found in many other aspects of intergovernmental relations in the United States. As the Project's state co-manager described it: "No place else in the world, when you have a fire do you have a federal fire department, a state fire department and a county fire department all respond, and then argue over who should be in charge or how you should go about fighting it. We have that model everywhere"[23]. Or as a senior USDA official put it more succinctly for the Project: "There was too much leadership at all levels: federal, state, and especially county. It was a mess..."[24].

One example from many illustrates how the interorganizational tension arising out of the Project's co-management influenced the way various parties perceived the risk associated with the various eradication proposals. Once aerial spraying began in July 1981 USDA took steps to prevent any recurrence of disputes such as that arising when members of the TAC had disagreed with USDA over the utility of the proposed 1980/81 winter spraying with malathion. After aerial spraying began, a permanent USDA co-manager was appointed to the Project (prior to that the federal co-managers had been rotated on a 30-day basis, itself a cause of a number of organizational problems in the operation of the Medfly Project). Equally important, the TAC was reconstituted to make it more favorably disposed to the aerial spraying program. Thereafter, the USDA exerted a much stronger influence on the running of the Project and its Technical Advisory Committee, according to the TAC's former chairperson. He went on to explain: "The Committee was revamped and [a USDA official] replaced me as the chairman. [He] was a good showman, a loyal soldier. He reported to the project leadership to find out what they wanted and he came in and sold it to the Committee. They put several other USDA people on the Committee; the most unfortunate choice was [a senior USDA official]...[whose beliefs were] based upon experience, not based upon scientific facts"[25]. This senior USDA official, in turn, happened to be the new chairperson's superior within the USDA hierarchy and a long-time advocate of aerial spraying with malathion for such infestations. In the view of the former TAC chairperson, this senior official "rammed...through" the committee what some of its members considered to be a very risky measure (namely, to consider the aerial spraying of a commodity with malathion sufficient for its export without any supplemental fumigation)[26]. Another TAC member described this effort in the following terms: "...we [on the TAC] were told very directly, 'I don't care what you decide you're going to recommend. We're going to do it this way"[27]. "I felt that [this senior USDA official], particularly, had an overall control of what came out of that Technical Committee" is how a newspaper reporter covering the operations of the TAC described the matter more generally[28].

USDA did not, however, present a united front in its approach to the eradication alternatives and the risks attached to them. Not surprisingly, "distrust" arose between staff within the research arm of USDA, the Agricultural Research Service (ARS), which had been an early developer and supporter of the SIT approach to fruit fly eradication, and staff within the applied arm of USDA, the Animal Plant Health Inspection Service (APHIS), which had a great deal of experience in and was a strong supporter of eradication programs based on aerial spraying of pesticides. The impact of such organizational differences on risk perceptions is well-illustrated in the dispute that arose over the aborted USDA proposal for winter spraying of malathion, where a well-known ARS entomologist on the TAC questioned the efficacy of this APHIS-originated proposal without first proving that the SIT-based ground program had been ineffective[29]. (APHIS officials were to later complain that had winter spraying taken place, the mid-1981 outbreak could have been avoided as well as many of the costs associated with it.)

*Intraprofessional Conflict.* Differences within professions and groups also filtered and structured the perceptions of risk. Perhaps the most notable example of this were the widely varying opinions expressed within the medical community about the recommendation against aerial spraying made by the pharmacology faculty at Stanford University, many of whom presumably worked or lived in the spray zones of Santa Clara Valley (see below). A number of other professional differences were also recorded. The Project's state co-manager recounted: "One member of the Technical Advisory Committee, a Ph.D. entomologist who had spent his whole life studying the medfly, said, 'Don't release [the sterile flies] by truck...Release them by plane.' Another member, also a Ph.D. with the same kind of background, said, 'Don't release them by plane...'"[30]. Someone familiar with the different factions in CDFA noted "One group [in the Department] said trapping was the only way to go, another group said 'biometric' grid surveys were the only way to go, and the third group said, 'I'll follow my nose to find larvae'"[31]. Finally, those who favored one of the two principal alternatives for treating the infestation were not always in agreement or necessarily in total opposition to the other proposal. Dr E.F. Knipling, considered to be the father of the sterile release technique, was "aghast that the area hadn't had aerial spraying before the sterile flies were released", according to one informed source[32].

*The Multiple Contexts And Sources of Conflict.* These differing views within professions and between professionals were not easily reconcilable within the existing organizational arrangements. For example, while the public advisory process frequently involves some compromises on the part of science experts, what was particularly troublesome to several of the scientists on the TAC was the specific committee procedure requiring them to vote and come to some kind of consensus on matters of science, principle and uncertainty, which they felt were by their very nature not votable. According to one of the TAC entomologists, such a procedural requirement tried to make medfly detection and eradication more certain than it was or could be:

...voting implies two things that are counterproductive to management and public understanding. First, it implies that the voter casts his ballot from a position of surety and conviction. Second, it implies that scientists differ on such points from positions of surety and conviction, which compromises the integrity of science. The truth usually is, however, that the data base is weak, the scientist unsure of his compromises...and his estimate of applicability of his experience to the problem at hand is questionable[33].

At times the differences between the various science advisors involved in the controversy were perceived to be less a matter of science than of personality, experience, or politics. A well-known university entomologist argued that, since "true objectivity and neutrality do not exist in science", those seeking technical advice could "more or less shop around and get the answers they desire"[34]. Some of those involved in the debate felt that scientists had "hidden agendas"[35]. Others were not so hidden: One member of the TAC was said to have "had a solid agenda [on the committee] and he didn't care if sterile flies worked or not. He wanted aerial bait sprays"[36]. A newspaper reporter covering many of the events over this period gave a number of examples of where she felt the TAC had made decisions and recommendations for political, rather than scientific, reasons: "On one hand, some would say, 'I am a scientist. Therefore, I have to have pure information before I can say anything.' The next thing, they'd turn around and do something that was just absolutely, blatantly political"[37]. Another perspective on this seeming equivocation was provided by one of the entomologist members of the TAC, "Sometimes we [i.e., members of the TAC] spoke up and said, 'Don't forget, these data are not so hot.' Other times we may have kept quiet, thinking, for example, 'Let them take the chance. Maybe it will work...'"[38].

Scientists were not the only group with varying views on the proposed solutions to the medfly infestations. Politicians differed considerably in terms of their support for either of the principal proposals to deal with the infestation. Political posturing was common: At least one state senator was accused of varying his position in the controversy, depending on what county he happened to be speaking in[39]. Similarly, environmentalists had political and organizational imperatives that complicated their support of the ground program and opposition to aerial spraying with malathion. For example, members of the main environmental action group involved in the controversy disagreed over whether or not to continue their support of the ground program after the mid-1981 medfly outbreak. The problem for them was that the eradication proposals and alternatives involved pesticides, the use of which the organization was nominally against as a matter of principle. As one of the representatives of this organization put the dilemma:

A lot of our members don't use pesticides in their gardens, yet we had been in the position of encouraging them to tolerate the repeated ground applications of pesticides. At that time I supported dropping our opposition to aerial sprays; however, the organization decided to continue to oppose aerial treatments, and we encouraged the Governor to go with the intensified ground program, even after the threatened federal quarantine which would have entailed substantial use of EDB [ethylene dibromide, the much more toxic and potent carcinogen used to fumigate potentially infested fruit for export]....Of course, [the many other members who opposed aerial spraying] are our major source of funds, and people speak with their pocket books...[40]

**Politics.**

Where bureaucratic and interest group politics ended and party politics began was not always obvious in the public debate over the 1980/82 California medfly infestation. Nonetheless the controversy took on a new dimension when it became embroiled in California state politics and that of the Nation's capital.

It is clear that Governor Brown's handling of the medfly crisis was one of several reasons why some state politicians and agribusiness interests sought to bring impeachment charges against him, seeking thereby to thwart his expected bid for the US Senate, among other things. It is less clear to what extent Brown's perceptions of the risks attached to the two major proposals for eradication were influenced by these and other political considerations. For example, Brown said he decided to expand the ground program in July 1981, even though he recognized "the serious political consequences" of doing so. "We have a pesticide," Brown noted about malathion,

that the Health department [DHS] says presents very little risk. Pharmacologists from Stanford and over 50 physicians say that it is dangerous and that there are possibly long-term effects, that there have been no long-term studies that can guarantee the safety of the aerial application of malathion...[41]

While this statement was made at a press conference justifying his decision to go ahead with the expanded ground program, Brown also appears to have privately expressed similar sentiments to his advisors: "Aerial [spraying] is not a guarantee...we are not dealing with an absolutely sure-fire program versus something that doesn't work. We are dealing with something that some people think will work as good. Other people think [it] will not work as good, and whatever we do we still have a risk and a problem"[42]. After working with him during this period, the Project's state co-manager came to a similar conclusion about the Governor's motivations: "I believe that Brown felt deeply that spraying with pesticide was wrong, no matter how he analyzed the problem he came back to that end and said, 'It is wrong and I don't care what the political risks are'"[43].

Yet some of these very same advisors paint a more complex picture of Brown and his actions. When the Project's state co-manager tried to impress upon the Governor how the decision not to go for aerial spraying, while it would appeal to Santa Clara residents, could well hurt his electoral chances with other California voters, Brown snapped "I'll worry about the politics, you worry about the medfly"[44]. And worry about the politics of medfly Brown did, at least according to the former Democratic chairperson of the California state assembly's agriculture committee who worked with him during this period:

After the helicopters were in the air [spraying malathion], some of us visited [the Governor] and advised, "Jerry, for God's sake, just stay out of it. Don't make another damn remark." But he thought the medfly was the hottest issue in the world at the moment and he wanted to capitalize on it for a while....I think Jerry, above all people, wanted eradication as soon as possible, because this was to his political gain. He knew he had an albatross around his neck if the ground program didn't work, but he didn't want aerial spraying because he felt that 90% of the people in the Santa Clara area would react negatively to helicopters flying over them....I think Jerry knew that he was going to have to order the helicopters into the air, but he wanted to cover himself and make it look like President Reagan forced him because they were going to quarantine the whole state.[45]

By this time, Brown had not endeared himself to the Reagan administration. It is accepted knowledge that the Project was denied the use of Moffett Field Air Station for the aerial spraying because of the Governor's comments about the President[46]. Only after enormous pressure from the state's Farm Bureau and other farm organizations on Secretary of Defense Weinberger did the Field become available for Project use[47]. These agricultural groups had exerted their political influence in Washington in other ways that worked against Brown's stated position in favor of the expanded ground program. In the judgment of the Project's federal co-manager, "the agribusiness interests [in California] are what finally triggered the aerial treatment" by bringing pressure on the Secretary of Agriculture to call for immediate aerial spraying in July 1981[48].

## The Media's Role in the Medfly Controversy.

"Jerry Brown received too much press..." is how the former chairperson of the state's agriculture committee summarized the difficulties the Governor found himself in at that time[49]. Indeed and more generally, the coverage of the controversy by the press, radio and television greatly influenced how many other people both saw the controversy and perceived the risks it raised. The two researchers who analyzed a community's perceptions of the risks associated with malathion spraying (to be discussed in the next section) summarized what were probably the impressions many had about the controversy at its high point. Our perceptions, they said,

of the circumstances as they were developing were highly influenced by what was presented in the press and television. The situation as we saw it was not unlike a Vietnam-style war--of attacks by helicopters and airplanes, taking off from unspecified areas, designated as top secret, with cargo highly-classified and toxic. The press informed us of guerilla-like activity from citizens actually taking up arms and shooting at the aircraft. Picket lines and sabotage of spraying operations were headline news, as well as intentional transportation of flies to uninfested areas. Coupled with this view of public response, we were reading how the medfly was out-smarting the entomologists and other scientists charged with ridding our state of the sneaky little pest..[50]

A brief flavor of these highly spiced events can be gotten from the headlines of a regional California newspaper during the two days it gave the most column inches to the 1980/82 medfly infestation: "Mighty Med--sneaky, persistent medfly juggernaut with a head start," "Motherhood and malathion," "All I can do is trust experts--and hope," "Resilient Medfly has broken all the rules," and "Human error made it easier"[51].

Many of the key participants to the controversy felt that the media's coverage of the issues it raised left much to be desired, particularly in the area of explaining the risks associated with the various eradication proposals. Some of their criticisms are doubtless self-serving, but worth quoting for their shared animus. "The press and the public never understood the difference between statistical confidence and personal confidence" felt one of the beleaguered science advisors on the TAC[52]. "I should have known this would happen because the press always picks up dissent" said the DHS official about the public controversy that followed when his concerns over the methodology of his department's risk assessment had been leaked to a newspaper[53]. The representative of the major environmental action group involved in the controversy claimed that he "was a little shocked" to find out that "the press would use a four or five month old press release [of his organization] for their articles," adding that the "press was predominately discussing the health hazards and concerns" when instead "about 75% of our press releases talked about the most effective way to deal with the pest"[54]. When asked "Do you think the press contributed generally to the sense of hysteria?" during the medfly controversy, a newspaper reporter who had covered these events for the state's best known newspaper answered, "I think they did"[55].

If the media abused, it was also used. Often the press reported only what it saw and heard at the public meetings of the Project and the TAC: Doomsayers in attendance frequently predicted the worst if aerially spraying went ahead or did not go ahead. One particularly important event illustrates how the media, instead of fanning the fires of public hysteria, was itself manipulated in such a way as to reduce the risks people perceived associated with aerial spraying. The decision of Project's state co-manager to allow the media open access to Project staff proved to be one of the decisive reasons why some members of the press were considerably less critical of the Project's first aerial spraying efforts in July 1981 than they could have been. According to the newspaper reporter mentioned earlier, the Medfly Project was in great turmoil on the day before aerial spraying commenced. One of her colleagues was running around trying to figure out how the spraying program would work. Since no one on the Project had time to provide an explanation, Project staff told him to sit in on their meetings and pick up what he could from what what was said. "He listened to everything," she said, adding

That would scare the beans out of 99% of the world's bureaucrats to let a reporter listen as they worked things out...That night, when they started spraying, the pumps broke...The AP put out a bulletin saying that the initial spraying had failed. Well, they weren't wrong. The pumps broke and they didn't get it sprayed; so, yes, they failed...[O]ur story was a little bit different. All it said was that they began the spraying but failed to complete it because a pump broke...[W]e gave them [i.e., the Project] the benefit of the doubt. Since we operate the Times-Post wire service, all of our client's readers got this story also. I felt our story was fair and accurate; and it happened because of the project's openness[56].

The Project's state co-manager described the events of that night and their implications for press coverage from a different perspective,

>...the pumps jammed closed and when the helicopter went over nothing came out. The press and public said, "Jesus, is that all there is to it? I thought there was going to be more than this." The news stories the next day said, "Is this all there is?" and overnight public reaction changed. [One major San Francisco newspaper] did a poll at the end of that week and 73% of the people were in favor of aerial spraying. The week before you couldn't have found two percent in favor....[T]he media was seduced by our candor. We let them have the run of the project. They got to talk to anybody they wanted to. I think they are not used to that, and as a result they were much more fair, even biased in our favor than you would normally find. There were a number of incidents where [Project] employees stole a vehicle and took the day off at the beach...or tipped over a spray rig. It was not a big story, because the media was living with us on this project. There was all this complexity and they said, "Well, hell, with this many people you are going to have those kinds of problems; that is not news."[57]

### The Public's Reaction[58].

Did, in fact, the media's changing coverage of the controversy have the kind of general effect just implied by the Project's state co-manager? What indeed were the public's perceptions of the risks associated with the ground and aerial spraying programs and how did these perceptions influence the public's actual behavior?

Two researchers at the University of California, Davis, undertook a telephone survey of 126 randomly selected persons in a town within Santa Clara County that had been subject both to the earlier ground program and the later aerial spraying with malathion. The survey took place during the first several months of aerial spraying and thus was able to assess how the number of sprayings affected risk perceptions of local residents.

Given the graphic media coverage described earlier by the researchers, they

>were particularly surprised, after our [survey] results were in, to find very little hostility [toward aerial spraying], and high acceptability of eradication by those sampled...This gave us pause to think that, perhaps,...the experts in Medfly eradication were also, in a way, duped by the press. Duped in the sense that public reaction was not as heated and considerably more supportive than what [we] were led to believe[59].

From what was said earlier, this finding should have not been all that surprising. The media responds to the "squawk factor" in its reporting of public meetings--those who shout the loudest frequently get the most coverage--and by and large the public are not squawkers. Still, the press was not without influence on its readers (particularly when it came to influencing environmental as distinct from health risk perceptions), as shall be seen momentarily.

The survey found that some 90% of the respondents relied on television or newspapers for information about the medfly situation in their area. Similarly, nearly all of the respondents (94%) felt the medfly provided a major threat to the California economy. The two basic alternatives to handling the medfly infestation met with a high degree of acceptance in the community: Of those responding, 86% agreed with the pesticide spraying component of the ground program (only 56% were in agreement with the sterile fly method), while 81% agreed with the aerial application of pesticides. Except for the sterile fly releases, about one-third of the respondents felt the eradication efforts were very effective, while around one-half ranked them as somewhat effective.

Some three-fourths (73%) of the respondents considered the ground spraying to be of slight or no risk to humans. Roughly two-thirds (66%) of the sample felt the same about aerial spraying. The majority of respondents considered the environmental problems of ground and aerial spraying to be minimal (66% and 62% perceived slight or no hazard, respectively).

However, what the sampled residents expressed about their perceptions of risk differed somewhat from the actual behavior they demonstrated in response to the perceived risks. Less than 10% of the sample reported taking none of the publicized precautions at all during aerial spraying. Approximately two-thirds of the sample (64%) said they had stayed indoors to avoid the aerial spraying; some three-quarters reported closing doors and windows; and slightly more than half (52%) of the sample kept children and pets inside. (The researchers did not say how unusual such precautionary behavior was at that time.) Work and jobs kept some people from taking the precaution that they wanted to, namely, leaving the area completely.

Based upon their reading of the relevant literature and taking as the dependent variables the sample's degree of perceived risk and the acceptability of such risk, the researchers hypothesized some nine important independent variables affecting both health and environmental risk perceptions of the sample and its acceptability of the risks assoicated with the spraying programs: the respondent's age, sex, education, political orientation, experience with or knowledge of pesticides, confidence in chemical industry experts, number of aerial sprayings, perceived benefit of eradication efforts, and response to media coverage, the latter being measured by his or her attitudes before and after the aforementioned two-day "media event" (when the column inches devoted to the medfly infestation increased by almost four times over the amount before and after this time in the regional newspaper concerned). Health and environmental risk perceptions, in turn, were also hypothesized to influence risk acceptability of a respondent. While approaching statistical significance in some cases, a number of the independent variables were found to be unreliable predictors. However, four variables were found to be reliable in predicting respondent variation in risk perceptions. To quote the researchers at length:

Those having the least confidence in industry experts expressed the highest degree of perceived risk, and conservatives perceived the least risk in the spraying situation, and the liberals perceived the most. The power of the press was clearly demonstrated as respondents question after the media event [i.e., after aerial spraying had begun] perceived considerably more environmental risk than those polled before the event. And finally, as predicted, those believing the eradication program was beneficial expressed little worry about the attendant risks, compared with those seeing no benefit...In order to further scrutinize these four predictors, each was examined a second time with the influence of the other three first extracted through statistical procedures. All of the significant predictors of the perception of health risk continued to be significant. However, the political ideology dropped out as a predictor of the perception of environmental risks. This suggests that political ideology operates only indirectly in influencing the perception of environmental risk, perhaps by influencing confidence in experts and perceived benefit...[60]

The researchers found that several variables explained variations in the respondents' acceptability of risks associated with the spraying programs. Again, to quote the researchers at length:

Those expressing less confidence in experts indicated less acceptability as well. Liberals were less accepting than conservatives. As perceived benefit increased, so did acceptability, and high health and environmental risk perception was associated with less acceptability...When each predictor was re-examined with all other significant predictors extracted, only perceived health risk and perceived environmental risk were significant predictors. This suggests that, in the present situation, acceptance was primarily influenced by one's opinion of the health and environmental hazards involved. Political ideology, confidence in experts, perceived benefits, and the media all influenced risk acceptability by influencing the perception of health risks. Nonetheless, both health and environmental risk perceptions contained variance unaccounted for by these other variables and both remained predictive when all other predictors were statistically controlled.[61]

Last but not least, only a few in the researchers' sample attributed illnesses to the chemical spraying, at least at the time of the survey. Some 2% and 6% of the respondents said they had become ill from the exposure to chemicals used in the ground and aerial spraying, respectively (the commonly reported symptoms were respiratory difficulties and nausea [25% each of those reporting ill] and headaches [13%]). These findings were confirmed by DHS research undertaken at roughly the same time in another part of Santa Clara County[62]. Asthma admissions to the emergency room of a major county hospital did not go up after aerial spraying commenced any more than did control injuries unrelated to such spraying. In addition, no changes in the frequency of such symptoms as respiratory difficulties, allergies, dermatologic disorders, eye complaints, organophosphate poisonings and anxiety were found at this hospital before and after aerial spraying. A DHS telephone survey to 60 randomly selected individuals in a spray area and a control area also came up with similar findings. Indeed, anxiety was found to have gone down after spraying when compared to before (14% of this DHS telephone sample in the spray area complained of anxiety prior to aerial spraying compared to 6.5% after spraying had commenced). As a DHS official put it: "The day following the aerial spraying, people came out in the morning; they weren't falling over dead; they were alive and everything was O.K. This was a lytic phenomeon: After the crisis passed, the frequency of symptoms falls off dramatically and then returns to the control or normal base line"[63].

**Conclusion.**

As we have seen, some found surprising the finding that the public's risk perceptions were very different in several respects from what one would have thought, given the impressions left by media accounts or the kinds of scientific uncertainties, organizational conflicts and politics described earlier. Perhaps an even more important aspect of the controversy was also contrary to these impressions: By a number of effectiveness measures, the intergovernmental Medfly Project was a success.

The 1980/82 Project was probably more expensive in terms of staff, time, and money than it need have been. Also, no one knows for certain that chronic, long-term illnesses have not resulted from the malathion spraying. Indeed, no one can prove that the expanded ground program would not have worked and that it was the Project's aerial spraying of malathion, and that alone, which led to the medfly's eradication, if indeed eradication was what actually happened. But for all that, the organizational capacity of the federal, state and county agencies to respond to the infestation, often on very short notice, was realized on an impressive scale. According to the Project's state co-manager, the Project had by its end released over four billion sterile medflies, ground sprayed and stripped the fruit from more than 100,000 urban backyards, aerially sprayed approximately 900,000 acres in 44 cities and 8 counties (counting multiple applications 10 million acres were said to have been sprayed), distributed some 2.1 million notices door-to-door or by mail, handled over 250,000 telephone calls on the Project hotlines, and inspected over 5 million vehicles at roadblocks[64]. Not unimportantly, state and federal officials both inside and outside the Medfly Project were also able to work out an agreed-upon plan for handling the next medfly infestation.

While such figures are only estimates, these events of the early 1980s record not only a controversy but also the intergovernmental capacity to overcome an initially serious underestimation of logistical problems connected with eradication. And government officials did so by planning, implementing and managing a rather complex, large-scale program that was, albeit costly, nonetheless successful in achieving the aims it had set for itself. In these times when what is often communicated about public health and environmental risks is government's inability to effectively deal with them, the 1980/82 medfly controversy provides a salutary reminder that this is not always so.

**Appendix: A Chronology of the Medfly Controversy*.**

5 June, 1980
  One medfly male found in a Los Angeles trap. Sent immediately to Sacramento for verification. Two males found in a Santa Clara trap. Sent to Sacramento third class mail and received 17 June.

6 June
  California Medfly Progect created. First CDFA Project leader for the Santa Clara infestation named 20 June.

25 June-July 5
  Fruit stripping and collection begins.

8 July
  Technical Review Committee, later known as Technical Advisory Committee, is created, consisting of scientists to advise and review Project operations.

17 July
  State quarantine established (approximately 96 square miles in Santa Clara Co. and 130 square miles in Los Angeles Co.).

22 July
  First sterile flies released. Ground spraying and aerial release of flies begin 1 August.

31 October
  The infested area in Santa Clara Valley has grown to 175.8 square miles.

24 November
  USDA reaches consensus that aerial spraying with malathion is necessary. Three days later USDA and CDFA discuss tremendous pressure being exerted by California growers and other states for aerial spraying.

3 December
  CDFA and USDA hold news conference to announce proposed aerial spraying with malathion. TAC minutes show its members divided over whether or not such spraying is warranted at this time.

8-9 December
  Four city councils and the Santa Clara Board of Supervisors vote to prohibit aerial spraying. A number of other cities do the same later in the month.

11 December
  CDFA agrees to hold off on aerial spraying in order to see if intensified ground program will work.

Mid-December
  Eradication achieved in LA County. The California State Department of Health Services publishes its report on health risks associated with the aerial spraying of malathion bait mixture.

23 June, 1981
    First medfly larvae collected since intensified ground spraying began. CDFA officials are, however, uncertain what caused this fresh outbreak.

7 July
    TAC holds emergency meeting and recommends aerial spraying.

8 July
    TAC members meet with Governor Brown and try to convince him to start aerial spraying at once. Instead, the Governor announces an expanded ground program to handle the new outbreak.

9-10 July
    US Secretary of Agriculture John Block threatens to quarantine the entire state of California if aerial spraying is not begun immediately. Governor Brown announces aerial spraying will commence on 14 July. (Spraying begins shortly after midnight of the 13th from a secret helicopter base established in a Los Altos Hills cemetary. Pressure for Governor Brown's impeachment mounts.)

16 July
    Texas, South Carolina, Mississippi and Florida impose quarantines restricting movement of specific California produce. Other state and international quarantines (particularly Mexico and Japan) follow later that month and the next. These quarantines are subsequently lifted through court action or by other bureaucratic channels.

August
    The TAC is reorganized and a permanent USDA co-manager to the Medfly Project is assigned.

21 September, 1982
    USDA and CDFA hold news conference to officially declare eradication. TAC holds final meeting. All regulatory measures are dropped.


* Abstracted primarily from the USDA and CDFA's <u>Medfly Eradication Project Chronology of Events, June 1980 - September 1982</u>.

**Endnotes.**

1. Jerry Scribner (1985), "The 1980 California Medfly Program: A View From Management--The State Perspective," pp. 1-2.

2. The draft volume is tentatively titled <u>A Fly in the Policy Soup: The 1980 California Medfly Program in Multiple Perspective</u>, H. Lorraine, P. Tannenbaum and M. Trow, editors. I would like to thank Percy Tannenbaum for his comments on an earlier draft of this paper.

3. Cost and coverage figures from Erik Larsen, "A Close Watch On U.S. Borders To Keep The World's Bugs Out," <u>Smithsonian</u>, June 1987, p. 110.

4. In reality, the eradication alternatives were not strictly either/or in nature: The aerial spraying program had a ground component and the ground program, some contended, should have had a preliminary aerial spraying phase, a point discussed later in the paper.

5. Jerry Scribner, page 13.

6. Quoted from Greg Rohwer (1985), "The View From Washington," page 20.

7. Donald Dilley (1985), "The Technical Advisory Committee: Use and Abuse," page 8.

8. See Hilary Lorraine (1985), "Medfly: An Historical Overview: Tag-Team Wrestling in the Technical Arena," page 10.

9. John Thurman (1985), "Medfly Politics," page 7.

10. Jerry Scribner, page 3.

11. For example, see Cherryl Churchill-Stanland (1985), "Quality Control: Management's Forgotten Resource," page 17.

12. Donald Dahlsten (1985), "The Scientist as a Source of Technical Advice to Large Action Programs," page 14.

13. Hilary Lorraine, "Medfly: An Historical Overview...," pp. 28-30.

14. Dick Jackson (1985), "A View From Management--The Federal Perspective," page 20.

15. Dick Jackson, pp. 12, 13.

16. Cherryl Churchill-Stanland, page 11.

17. Derrell Chambers (1985), "Technical Advisors: Wise Men, Wizards, Wind Vanes or Wimps," pp. 5, 10.

18. Marc Lappé (1985), "Technical Dissent," page 9.

19. Marc Lappé, page 10.

20. Kathleen Rassbach (1985), "A Medical Overview of the Health Debate," pp. 9ff.

21. Quoted from the Rohwer chapter, page 24.

22. Steve Dreistadt (1985), "A View From The Community," page 9.

23. Jerry Scribner, page 1.

24. Greg Rohwer, page 8.

25. Donald Dilley, pp. 15-16.

26. Donald Dilley, page 16.

27. Derrell Chambers, page 19.

28. Tracy Wood (1985), "Medfly and the Media," page 27.

29. See Greg Rohwer, pp. 18-19.

30. Jerry Scribner, page 4.

31. Quoted from the Jackson chapter, page 11.

32. Quoted from the Rohwer chapter, page 21.

33. Derrell Chambers, page 21.

34. Donald Dahlsten, page 1.

35. Quoted from the Jackson chapter, page 23.

36. Quoted from the Churchill-Stanland chapter, page 25.

37. Tracy Wood, page 12.

38. Derrell Chambers, pp. 17-18.

39. John Thurman, page 11.

40. Steve Dreistadt, pp. 7, 8.

41. Quoted from Hilary Lorraine (undated), "Man the Master or Sorcerer's Apprentice," page 24.

42. Quoted from Hilary Lorraine, "Man the Master...," page 23.

43. Jerry Scribner, page 28.

44. Jerry Scribner, page 27. Such a remark as the Governor's is not unusual. "You give me the perfect plan and I'll worry about the politics," so said President Carter to his HEW Secretary during the design of their ill-fated welfare reform proposal (Lawrence Lynn and David Whitman [1981], The President as Policymaker: Jimmy Carter and Welfare Reform, Temple University

Press, Philadelphia, page 89). Perhaps one of the best indices of a high-risk public policy issue is finding some of its key actors maintaining the commonplace distinction between politics and administration, when in reality that issue is so complex and uncertain as to blur the line between the two.

45. John Thurman, pp. 12, 14, 15.

46. Quoted from the Jackson chapter, page 17.

47. John Thurman, page 8.

48. Dick Jackson, page 16.

49. John Thurman, page 12.

50. Glenn Hawkes and Martha Stiles (1985), "A Survey of the Public's Assessment of Risk," page 3. Such dramatic events in the controversy also provided more personal forms of risk communication. "One evening [after aerial spraying had commenced] I rode with the Highway Patrol observation heliocopter," recalled the former chairperson of the state assembly's agriculture committee. "I asked, 'What are those flashes of light coming up through the air?' The Highway Patrolman said, 'Those are bullets.' I am not a coward but I said, 'Please, land this damn thing!'" (John Thurman, page 8).

51. Glenn Hawkes and Martha Stiles, page 4.

52. Derrell Chambers, page 11.

53. Marc Lappé, page 17.

54. Steve Dreistadt, page 12.

55. Tracy Wood, page 24.

56. Tracy Wood, page 8.

57. Jerry Scribner, pp. 11, 33-34.

58. Unless otherwise stated, all figures provided in this section are drawn from the Hawkes and Stiles chapter.

59. Glenn Hawkes and Martha Stiles, page 3.

60. Glenn Hawkes and Martha Stiles, page 17.

61. Glenn Hawkes and Martha Stiles, pp. 17-18.

62. Ephraim Kahn and Richard Jackson (1985), "Assessment of the Health Risks from the Proposed Aerial Application of Malathion in Santa Clara County," pp. 18-22.

63. Ephraim Kahn and Richard Jackson, pp. 21-22.

64. Jerry Scribner, page 12.

# COMMUNICATING CORPORATE DISASTER

## The Aldicarb Oxime Release at the Union Carbide Plant at Institute, West Virginia on August 11, 1985

Rob Coppock

The escape of a cloud of toxic gas from Union Carbide's Institute, West Virginia plant created far less hazard than did the methyl isocyanate gas leak in Bhopal, India the December before. But occurring as it did in the Bhopal spotlight--and just months after the company declared that a Bhopal-like disaster could not happen at the Institute plant--the accident dealt a heavy blow to the company's credibility with the public.

The release occurred on Sunday morning at 9:24. About 10:00 a.m., the County Office of Emergency Services activated its emergency siren at Institute. Hospital emergency facilities treated 134 people, and 28 were hospitalized.

The following Friday, August 16th, was the formal announcement of the creation of the National Institute for Chemical Studies (NICS) in Charleston, state capital of West Virginia and Kanawha County seat. NICS had been created by business, academic, and government leaders to serve as a bridging organization between business and the general public. Its activities have influenced subsequent events.

On the day of the accident, and throughout the following week, Union Carbide officials conducted a series of press conferences. The following describes these communications, the context within which they took place, and such information as is available regarding their impact.

## BACKGROUND[1]

The Kanawha valley, named for the Kanawha River which carved it, is one of just a few flat areas of West Virginia. Charleston, the state capital and the county seat of Kanawha County, is located at the confluence of the Elk River and the Kanawha. Before the first white settlers arrived, Native American Indians refined brine to make salt for food preservation at the site, and it was the presence of this and other chemical resources that stimulated settlement. By 1807, 52 salt furnaces were in operation along the Kanawha River.

The salt, oil, gas, and coal that are still plentiful in the area were attracting interest by the late 1800s as the basis for other chemical production. Shortly after the turn of the century, chlorine and caustic were being produced from brine. When World War I cut off chlorine and alkali supplies from Germany, production in the Kanawha Valley increased in importance. The war also resulted in construction of a naval ordinance plant and a plant devoted to making nitrocellulose for gunpowder.

In 1920, Union Carbide constructed a plant about 25 miles north, and moved to its present location in South Charleston in 1925. DuPont also built its plant in Belle in 1925. Since then, chemical production in the valley has continued to expand. Currently, the following facilities involving hazardous chemicals operate in Kanawha Valley: FMC, Nitro; Monsanto; Kincaid; Artel: PB&S Chemical; FMC, Institute: Union Carbide, Institute; Rhone-Polenc; Union Carbide, South Charleston; Olin; FMC, Spring Hill; Union Carbide Technical Center; DuPont; and Occidental.

The greater Charleston area has a population of about 250,000. In contrast to much of West Virginia, the area has an unemployment rate that is about equal to the national average. The residents are generally aware that the chemical industry has an excellent safety record, especially compared to the coal industry--another major employer in the state. In 1986, 18 people died in the coal mines and more than 1100 were injured. The other major employers in Charleston are state government and medicine.

In principle, the community can be divided into three groups with different needs and fears: people living adjacent to chemical plants for whom emergency response is the dominant concern; residents who are somewhat concerned about chronic effects of long-term exposure to emissions; and those who see the chemical industry principally as the provider of jobs and are supportive of it. However, there is some blurring of the borders separating these categories, especially the latter two.

## THE ALDICARB OXIME EMERGENCY

In December 1984, a Union Carbide production plant in Bhopal, India was the site of a leak of methyl isocyanate gas that resulted in about 2000 deaths and estimates of as many as several hundred thousand injuries. Union Carbide also produced methyl isocyanate, or MIC, at a sister plant in Institute, West Virginia. In response to this event, Union Carbide altered its operations at the plant in Institute.

The company stopped production of MIC-based pesticides for five months following the Bhopal incident. It spent about five million dollars improving safety measures in the MIC unit before it resumed operation in May 1985.

Previously, Union Carbide had produced MIC in Institute and shipped it to Woodbine, Georgia, where it was combined with aldicarb oxime, purchased from Allied Corporation, to produce aldicarb. Aldicarb is the active ingredient in Temik, a Union Carbide pesticide. In May 1985, Union Carbide shifted aldicarb production to Institute to avoid the need to ship MIC. Aldicarb was now shipped in solution to Woodbine, where it was formulated into Temik.[2]

Production of aldicarb had begun in a unit originally built for other service, which was scheduled to be replaced by a new, larger system. But on August 11, about 3800 pounds of material were expelled from a reactor being used as a storage vessel. Union Carbide chemists and engineers concluded that an exothermic decomposition of aldicarb oxime was the most likely cause of the eruption. The material expelled included about 650 pounds of methylene chloride solvent, 300 pounds of solid residue in pipes from previous use of the reactor, and only 8 pounds of aldicarb oxime. Other materials expelled were carbon monoxide, carbon dioxide, and sulfur compounds.[3] A detailed account of the accident may be found in Appendix A.

The release occurred at 9:24 a.m. Within 60 seconds, the plant alarm was activated. At 9:35 a.m., the Kanawha County Office of Emergency Services was advised of the release and that the material was, at that time, not identified. Ambulance service was requested because control room operators had been overcome. Due to an error in the computer telephone log at the Union Carbide plant, this communication was recorded as occurring at 9:44 a.m. This error resulted in confusion and later criticism. At 9:56 a.m., a deputy sheriff arrived and remained at the Plant Emergency Center throughout the emergency. Some individuals recall hearing the County emergency siren at this time, indicating that it was activated before 10:00 a.m. By 10:15 a.m., Union Carbide concluded that the release contained a mixture of aldicarb oxime, dichloromethane, carbon monoxide, carbon dioxide and sulfur compounds and the plant physician had completed contact to all area hospitals.[4]

The plume of toxic materials drifted beyond the plant boundaries into a nearby residential area and across the river to a shopping center. One hundred thirty-four people were treated at hospital emergency facilities, 28 were hospitalized, 6 of whom were Union Carbide employees, with 2 remaining in the hospital more than 5 days.

**UNION CARBIDE COMMUNICATIONS**

The toxic material escaped on Sunday morning, when few supervisors were in the plant. The air was hot and heavy, with little or no wind. Within minutes after the release, the shift supervisor employed a computerized simulation program to predict the likely spread of the plume. Not knowing the exact material released, he used MIC as a surrogate. The simulation program predicted that the plume would not cross the boundaries of the plant, and initial communication to the county emergency office did not indicate the need for evacuation or other community response.

About 20 minutes after the plant alarm, the assistant plant manager arrived. Shortly after this, the deputy sheriff arrived and state police began setting up roadblocks. By this time the plume had drifted over the plant boundaries and the public alarm had been sounded.

By 1:00 p.m., ABC News, CBS News, NBC News, Reuters, and the Today Show had contacted Union Carbide. At about 2:00 p.m., the plant manager met with the regional director of public affairs. In consultation with the head office in Danbury, Connecticut, a press release was prepared. It is attached as Appendix C. The State Pollution Control Commission was also informed.

A second press conference was held the next day in the parking lot of the Institute plant. It was prepared with the intention of addressing the questions of the exact materials that had been released and the time that had elapsed before county officials were contacted. It is attached as Appendix D.

By Tuesday, the second day after the emergency, reports were appearing in the national press criticizing another aspect of Union Carbide's actions. The plant physician had told area hospitals that aldicarb oxime was a very minor irritant that would have no long-term effects, but the company had classified the substance in the most toxic of four categories in a memo submitted to a Congressional subcommittee the year before.[5] Hazards associates with the materials released are described in Appendix B.

That day, Union Carbide's regional director of public affairs conducted a third press conference (see Appendix E). His statement went into greater detail about the properties of aldicarb oxime than had previous ones, and announced that a special committee on Safety, Health and Environmental Affairs, established by the company in January 1985 and chaired by Russell Train, President of the U.S. World Wildlife Fund, would conduct an independent investigation of the emergency. Senator Byrd and U.S. Environmental Protection Agency Administrator Lee Thomas toured the plant.

On Friday, August 16, Union Carbide Chairman Warren Anderson conducted a press conference at which he pledged that the company would speed up its warnings of leaks. "From now on," he said, "we will pull the cord first, than apologize if it wasn't necessary." (See the press release attached as Appendix F.) The press conference was scheduled in part to remove discussion of the Union Carbide emergency from the press conference announcing the establishment of NICS.

On Sunday, August 18, about 350 people attended a meeting at West Virginia State College, whose campus abuts the Union Carbide Institute plant. It was attended by the Union Carbide president, the regional director of public relations, and the plant manager.

**MAJOR INFLUENCES ON UNION CARBIDE'S COMMUNICATIONS**

Union Carbide's communications about the aldicarb oxime emergency described above can be divided into roughly three separate concerns: activation of county and other emergency response organizations, informing exposed individuals and reassuring local residents, and maintenance of the reputation of the company and its ability to do business (avoiding lawsuits, for example, or countering lower prices for its stocks).

There was tension between three conflicting perspectives--a conflict that probably exists for corporate communications about any emergency. First and foremost were the legal ramifications. After the initial emergency response, when the overriding concern is what to do to contain and stop the emergency, almost every business person immediately wonders who will bring suit. Legal advice is almost always to give out as little information as possible so as to avoid providing ammunition for use in court. This is in almost direct conflict with what communications and community relations experts advise, which is to say everything you know, as quickly as possible, in terms the layperson can easily understand. Somewhere in the middle is the scientific and engineering perspective, which cautions against attributing cause-and-effect before being reasonably certain what happened. They prefer to say as little as possible until being sure about the course of events. Whatever message is finally sent out will probably involve a compromise among these three perspectives.

One result is that at Union Carbide, like most large corporations, almost all formal communications are carefully vetted. Pre-approved information sheets provide data on toxicity of various materials, and the contents of the two initial press statements were approved by the corporate headquarters via telephone. By Tuesday, when more detail was presented, communications experts from corporate headquarters and local public relations consultants were involved.

A second major influence on the content of Union Carbide's press statements was the treatment of the emergency by the press. This attempt to be responsive to the needs of reporters, however, can backfire. For example, the initial statements indicated that the release included both aldicarb oxime and dichloromethane. The press, however, devoted its attention almost exclusively to aldicarb oxime and the discrepancy between the plant physician's description of the material as a minor irritant and its classification by Union Carbide in its most toxic category. Subsequent statements by Union Carbide went into detail about the toxicity of aldicarb oxime. Sometime later in the week, about Thursday, a reporter accused Union Carbide of trying to cover up the fact that dichloromethane was also released.

## THE MEDIA

A detailed examination of press treatment is beyond the scope of this paper. At least sixty-nine articles related to the emergency appeared during the first week. However, the following opinions seem to be shared by Union Carbide personnel, employees of other chemical companies, and local officials with whom I spoke.

Many individuals in the Kanawha Valley feel that Union Carbide has been unfairly treated by the national press as a result of the Bhopal affair. One company employee felt that national reporters came to town to gather support for a story they had already written rather than to find out what happened. Nearly everyone I spoke to characterized local news as having a better understanding of regional economics and the chemical industry.

The now-deceased editor of one of the two Charleston-based newspapers had a policy of "sustained outrage" in his paper. It reputedly challenged government and industry consistently about pollution and similar problems. But both papers are viewed as dealing with the emergency more fairly and more knowledgeably than the national press.

As has been observed with respect to other issues,[6] the local and regional press included more "human interest" stories. Interviews of the first residents to have detected the release, a song about the release written by a local disc jockey, plant workers sharing oxygen masks during the emergency, a canvass showing the sirens failed to warn most residents--these are stories that probably lack lasting appeal beyond the local or regional area.

## COMMUNITY ATTITUDES

In principle, the community can be divided into three groups with different needs and fears: people living adjacent to chemical plants for whom emergency response is a dominant concern; residents who are somewhat concerned about chronic effects of long-term exposure to emissions; and residents who see the chemical industry principally as the provider of jobs and are supportive of it. However, there is some blurring of the borders separating these categories, especially the latter two.

In late spring 1985, before the emergency described in this paper, NICS initiated an activity designed to assess the views of residents in the Kanawha Valley on the benefits and environmental risks of living in the Valley. The Public Agenda Foundation, a nonpartisan, nonprofit research and education organization located in New York City, was asked to undertake a two-part project. Phase one consisted of six focused group interviews with residents, chemical plant workers, and community activists held in August and September. The second phase consisted of a survey of public opinion later that fall.

The focused group interviews suggested that the August 11 leak and the subsequent events were polarizing public opinion between chemical workers, on the one hand, and accident victims, on the other.[7] A series of hypotheses developed from these focused group interviews are presented in Appendix G.

Phase two tested the hypotheses developed in the initial phase.[8] The principal findings of the survey are:

- People in the Valley have a reservoir of good will toward the chemical companies;

- People in the Valley want a sound economy and safe environment but currently feel they have neither one, nor are they optimistic that conditions in the Valley will improve in the future;

- People are willing to make certain trade-offs in order to improve the economy and environment, but only within limits, and not generally at a risk to their health or by rolling back environmental regulations;

- While people believe that the industry has helped to improve the environment in the Valley, they question the companies' commitment to reducing health hazards, and they don't entirely trust them as reliable sources of information; and

- Although residents are generally well informed, many people have little trust in the information sources available in the Valley.

The report on phase two includes the following conclusion:

> When the Public Agenda began its research in the Kanawha Valley, in August of 1985, it was by coincidence that the Union Carbide incident occurred at Institute. It was striking that at that time public attitudes in the Valley, at least in the focused group discussions, did not appear to shift dramatically against the chemical industry. Nevertheless, because residents do not entirely trust chemical company spokespersons or other information sources and because of the clear concern for the environment revealed in the survey, one cannot be confident that public attitudes in the Valley will remain where they are today. It is the Public Agenda's sense that another leak or accident--one perhaps not even in the Valley--could turn current public attitudes which appear to be relatively stable into a more volatile, perhaps even hostile, state.

The most vocal of those living adjacent to the thirteen chemical plants in the Valley appear to be those living in Institute. This may reflect an underlying racial issue. The residents of Institute are predominantly black, and the State College was originally a Negro teachers college (current enrollment is about 85% white, matching the figure for the West Virginia population as a whole). Unlike other communities bordering chemical plants, residents in Institute cannot count employees of the plant among their numbers. Until only a few years ago, the company did not hire blacks. Not only does the lack of "neighbor-spokesman" mean that the firm's position is not represented in the community, but there appears to be a residual feeling of distrust and hostility toward the company's previous policies.

On August 18, 1985, just a week after the aldicarb oxime release, about 350 people attended an emotional meeting at West Virginia State College, whose campus abuts the Union Carbide plant. The meeting was sponsored by "People Concerned About MIC," a citizens' organization, and was attended by Robert Kennedy, President of Union Carbide. A year later, about 50 people met at a quieter meeting to remember the event and assess change.[9] At the first meeting, Kennedy promised improvements in emissions, and by the next year they had been reduced by 30 percent. At the 1985 meeting, a Union Carbide employee accused the company of manning the plant with undertrained personnel. A year later, the same person believed that a new safety training program had resulted in greater safety. Questions about the extent of injuries that would have occurred had the college been in session, as opposed to the actual event with occurred on a Sunday morning, have yet to be resolved. Although an additional evacuation route has been built, some believe another access ramp to the interstate highway is needed.

People who live adjacent to the chemical plants and for whom emergency action is the greatest concern probably number in the hundreds. Those who are primarily concerned about chronic effects probably number in the several thousands. The remaining hundreds of thousand residents of the Valley probably see the chemical industry as the provider of jobs and are supportive of it.

## RESULTING CHANGES IN UNION CARBIDE POLICY AND PROCEDURES

Several changes appear to have been instituted in Union Carbide as a result of this emergency. The company claims to have reduced the degree of judgment allowed personnel in the decision of when to initiate communications with emergency response organizations outside its plants. It aims at being more conservative, to err on the side of rapid and immediate communication.

The company also claims to have initiated more intensive audits of safety procedures in its plants. Internal audit teams review the procedures developed by plant managers. In addition, community emergency response organizations employing more sophisticated control centers, such as that in St. Charles Parish, Louisiana, have been examined.

Finally, a series of regional meetings with plant managers was organized. These were two day seminars covering topics such as how to deal with print and electronic media, how to identify and use information resources, and how to establish rapport with local media and civic leaders.

## NOTES

1. The material in this section relies on an anonymous paper titled "Chemical Reactions in the Kanawha Valley of West Virginia" distributed to participants at the National Institute for Chemical Studies conference "Living with Chemicals: Communicating the Risks, Benefits, and Choices," March 11-13, 1987.

2. "Union Carbide: New Accidents Revive Safety Issues," Chemical and Engineering News, August 19, 1985, p.4.

3. "Carbide Restructures: Problems Prompt Massive Cutbacks," Chemical and Engineering News, September 2, 1985, p.7.

"Union Carbide: New Accidents Revive Safety Issues," Chemical and Engineering News, August 19, 1985, p.5.

4. Based on an interview with Thad Epps on May 18, 1987, and on a Union Carbide press statement dated August 12, 1985.

5. Stuart Diamond, "Carbide Blames a Faulty Design for Toxic Leak; Effects Can Be Serious, Company Memo Says," New York Times, August 13, 1985, pp.A1, B8.

6. See, for example, Harold I. Sharlin, "EDB: A Case Study in the Communication of Health Risk," report to the Office of Policy Analysis, U.S. Environmental Protection Agency, Washington, D.C., January 9, 1985.

7. The Public Agenda Foundation, "Public Chemistry--A Report on the Feasibility of a Communications Project for the Kanawha Valley," The Public Agenda Foundation, New York, undated.

8. The Public Agenda Foundation, "The Kanawha Valley: A Report on Public Attitudes Toward Economic Benefits and Environmental Risks," The Public Agenda Foundation, New York, January 1986.

9. Mike Towle, "Carbide Neighbors View Leak As Catalyst For Change," Charleston Daily Mail, August 8, 1986, p.1-A.

## APPENDIX A

### THE CHRONOLOGY OF EVENTS

(based on: "Carbide Restructures: Problems Prompt Massive Cutbacks," <u>Chemical and Engineering News</u>, September 2, 1985, p.7.)

As Union Carbide investigators reconstruct the incident, methylene chloride was piped into the aldicarb reactor on August 1. Aldicarb oxime was introduced next. A malfunction in a flow meter caused too much oxime to be let in. Engineers installed a temporary pipeline to pump the solution into another 5000 gallon, glass-lined reactor that had not been used since 1984.

Unknown to the operators, steam flowed into the jacket of this reactor from August 1 to 7. The heat caused methylene chloride (boiling point 104°F) to boil off from the oxime (boiling point 410°F), raising the concentration of oxime from 38 percent to 81 percent. Methylene chloride was later found to have condensed in two connected vessels called the knock-out pot and the crystallizer.

Not realizing that this change had occurred, Union Carbide operators tried to pump the reactor contents back into the aldicarb reactor on August 7. After two and a half hours, the pump appeared not to be moving any more material, and it was shut off. Operators could not use level indicators to determine that the pumping was incomplete because the remaining 500 gallons formed what is called a heel in the convex bottom of the vessel.

Steam continued to flow into the reactor jacket, and the temperature rose. To know that this was happening, operators would have had to call up the display of the reactor's condition on the control room computer. Thinking the reactor empty, they did not do this.

From laboratory experiments and computer simulations, Union Carbide investigators conclude that on the morning of August 11 the reactor temperature reached 300°F. This initiated exothermic decomposition of the oxime. At 9:25 a.m., a differential pressure alarm went off, indicating that a safety valve had burst and that a high flow of gas was flowing through the knock-out pot and scrubber to the flare tower. An operator entering the control room heard a rumbling sound from the reactor. He looked toward the flare tower and saw a lot of smoke. After four seconds, the differential pressure indicator dropped precipitously, indicating that other release valves had opened. The plant alarm was sounded at 9:26 a.m.

An opaque, white fume engulfed the yard and control room, trapping five operators and their foreman. The men could not see the panels in front of them. At 9:32 a.m. the eruption ended. A minute later the workers were led to safety. At 9:36 a.m. county officials were notified. By 10:00 a.m., a public warning siren had been sounded.

## APPENDIX B

### HAZARDS ASSOCIATED WITH THE MATERIALS

(based on: "Union Carbide: New Accidents Revive Safety
Issues," Chemical and Engineering News, August 19, 1985, p.5)

The principal materials released were methylene chloride solvent, aldicarb oxime, carbon dioxide and monoxide, and sulfur compounds. The principal hazards were associated with methylene chloride, which made up the bulk of the cloud, and aldicarb oxime.

Methylene chloride, which boils at 104°F, is nonflammable, and its mixtures with air are not explosive. The $LD_{50}$ (dose that kills 50% of experimental animals) of methylene chloride is 1.6 ml per kg in rats. EPA considers methylene chloride to be a potential carcinogen on the basis of one recent study.

Aldicarb oxime is a high-boiling liquid that melts at 70°F and boils at 410°F. Its vapor pressure is less than 0.1 torr at 70°F. The oxime is an irritant to eyes, skin, and nasal passages. Union Carbide says its $LD_{50}$ is one tenth that of MIC, and does not believe exposure to the substance to have any long-term health effects, even though it classifies the substance in its "most hazardous" category.

Because of the lack of extensive health effect studies on aldicarb oxime, West Virginia Health Department officials will conduct a long-term study of all 135 people hospitalized after the exposure.

AGRICULTURAL PRODUCTS COMPANY, INC.

P.O. BOX 2831, CHARLESTON, WEST VIRGINIA 25330

INSTITUTE PLANT

FOR IMMEDIATE RELEASE
August 11, 1985

Institute, WV-- At 9:35 this morning the Union Carbide plant at Institute experienced a release of a mixture of aldocarb oxime, dichloromethane, carbon monxide, carbon dioxide and sulfur compounds. A preliminary investigation indicates a gasket failed because of a pressure buildup in a reactor being used as a storage tank. It is estimated the vessel contained approximately 500 gallons of material, the maximum amount which could have been released. However, much of the material was neutralized through venting to a scrubber and flare. An immediate investigation will be made to establish the cause of the accident and the quantity of material released.

Exposure to these materials can cause respiratory discomfort, vomiting, nausea and eye irritation. It is not expected that exposure would cause any long term affects. Six Union Carbide employees were hospitilized and are under 24 hour observation as a precautionary measure. The Institute plant physician contacted area hospital emergency rooms within 40 minutes of the incident to indicate appropriate treatment for exposure.

The plant notified the County Office of Emergency Services of the incident within approximately five minutes and recommended initiation of the first stages of the emergency response plan.

APPENDIX D

## UNION CARBIDE PRESS CONFERENCE STATEMENT AUGUST 12, 1985

August 12, 1985

There are three specific areas I want to cover.

First, the situation with the 28 people who were hospitalized, second the status of our investigation and the fact that no MIC was involved, and third the misconception that the Institute Plant did not respond in quick, timely fashion to this incident.

Fifteen of the 28 people hospitalized yesterday were released earlier today. More are expected to be released later today or tomorrow. All 13 who remain hospitalized are in satisfactory condition. We have no reason to believe that there will be any long term health affects.

In all, 134 people were seen at hospital emergency rooms, according to hospital officials who have spoken with our plant physician.

Union Carbide Corporation will assume responsibility for medical expenses for all 134 people.

Second, a team has been formed to fully investigate the leak of material from a plant storage tank early Sunday morning. Representatives of several regulatory agencies such as the West Virginia Air Pollution Control Commission, EPA, Department of Natural Resources and OSHA are in the plant.

Further inspection of the tank Monday confirms earlier reports that there were about 500 gallons of aldicarb oxime/dichloromethane mixture in the tank. It is now suspected the material overheated when steam entered a jacket on the storage tank resulting in a pressure build-up. This caused three gaskets on the tank to fail. In addition, a safety valve on the tank opened and discharged material into an emergency vent system. Further investigation showed that a rupture disc in the emergency system also opened discharging material to the atmosphere. We re-emphasize there was no MIC released in the incident.

The third thing I want to talk about is Union Carbide's response to this emergency situation. I want to <u>emphasize</u> that the Institute Plant followed the emergency response procedures devised by the Institute-West Dunbar-Pinewood Community Sub-Area Planning Council and adopted by the Kanawha Valley Emergency Planning Council (KVEPC). We were efficient in our reaction. We were timely with our response.

PRESS STATEMENT
Page Two

Here's the chronology of events:

— At 9:24 a.m. there was a release. Within 60 seconds, the plant alarm was activated and our emergency squad responded. At that time, we did not believe the emergency affected the community because the cloud was hovering over the plant. Later, our SAFER System indicated the cloud would move in a southwesterly direction.

— At 9:44 a.m., we advised the Kanawha County Office of Emergency Services that there had been a release and that we were not able to, at that moment, identify the material. We also advised them at that time that we needed ambulance assistance because control room operators had been overcome.

— Later, and, we believe, before 10:00 a.m., the County Office of Emergency Services activated its emergency siren at Institute.

— At 9:56 a.m, a Deputy Sheriff arrived at our plant and was escorted immediately to our Plant Emergency Center where he remained throughout the emergency.

— By 10:15 a.m,, we determined that the release contained a mixture of aldicarb oxime, dichloromethane, carbon monoxide, carbon dioxide and sulfur compounds and our plant physician had completed contact to all area hospitals to communicate appropriate treatment for exposure.

0341T

Update statement 10 a

A Union Carbide spokesman stated today that of the 28 people hospitalized because of exposure to the gas release at Union Carbide's plant in Institute, W. Va. yesterday, two have been released this morning according to the hospitals.

The others are in satisfactory condition without any signs of permanent injury.

The spokesman stated that the emergency response system worked according to plan and all government authorities and hospital emergency rooms were notified in a timely fashion.

The spokesman stated that the unit involved contained aldicarb oxime, not methyl isocyanate.

An investigation of the cause of the incident is under way by Union Carbide, and Federal and state agencies will also conduct their investigations.

APPENDIX E

# STATEMENT BY THAD EPPS*
## AUGUST 13, 1985 – UNION CARBIDE INSTITUTE PLANT

This morning I would like to cover the following points: hospital status of employees and residents involved in the accidental release of aldicarb oxime on Sunday, Aug. 11; steps we are taking to help ensure a similar incident can be avoided in the future; clarify some aspects of the incident itself; and comments on the community emergency response system as we see it.

As of this morning, 15 persons remain hospitalized, one of which is a Union Carbide employee. We expect that at least two additional poeple will be released today including our employee; the remainder are in satisfactory condition and will remain in the hospital a bit longer under observation.

While I believe most of you are aware of this, I would like to repeat that the chemical methyl isocyanate was <u>not</u> involved in this incident. Aldicarb oxime was. It is a product that is not made from MIC. It is later reacted with MIC to produce aldicarb.

The initial production of aldicarb at Institute occurred in May 1985 in a small existing unit. Aldicarb solution has been manufactured by Union Carbide at three locations – Woodbine, France, and Brazil, for the equivalent of over 20 years of safe plant operation. A new and larger aldicarb solution system has been in startup at Institute. The incident occurred in the smaller system which was in the process of being phased out. In view of the need for a complete understanding of the exact circumstances which led to the incident we have decided to temporarily suspend all aldicarb solution manufacture at Institute.

*Thad Epps is the Regional Director of Community Relations for Union Carbide

This morning, Warren M. Anderson, Chairman of Union Carbide Corporation, recommended to the Board of Directors and the Board has agreed that a special committee on Safety, Health and Environmental Affairs established in January 1985 and chaired by Russell Train, will conduct an independent investigation of the incident. It is expected that the investigation will involve outside consultants and an external peer review. Further, Union Carbide is committed to cooperating with all appropriate local, state and federal authorities. The temporary suspension of operations of the aldicarb units at Institute will affect the routine assignments of approximately 60 employees at Institute and another 240 employees at the company's Woodbine plant.

To clarify some aspects regarding the incident on Sunday, let me explain our statement of Monday regarding what we do know about the source of the emission: It is now suspected that about 500 gallons of aldicarb oxime/dichloromethane mixture in a tank overheated when steam entered a jacket on the storage tank resulting in a pressure build-up. This caused three gaskets on the tank to fail. In addition, a safety valve on the tank opened and discharged material into an emergency vent system. Furtherinvestigation showed that a rupture disc in the emergency system also opened dischargning material to the atmosphere. We re-emphasize there was no MIC released in the incident.

Regarding the toxicity of aldicarb oxime, there have been some reports suggesting that it is equal to methyl isocyanate. It is not. Union Carbide's toxicological information shows that MIC's toxicity, based upon $LD_{50}$ acute tests on oral, dermal, and inhalation applications, is about ten times that of aldicarb oxime. It is true that we rate both as a number four (4) for Union Carbide's rating system of individual chemcial's potential health effects. The number four indicates that all due precaution must be taken. However, within that category there are varying degrees of risk, with aldicarb oxime being on the low side and MIC being on the high side.

Finally, I would like to discuss the concern raised by some that the amount of time that elapsed between the occurrence of the incident and the activation of the emergency response plan might have been too long. Under the circumstances of this particular incident, we believe the time lapse was understandable. Nonetheless, we believe that there is, indeed, amiguity between public and private authorities as to who make those decisions to activate the emergency response plan that results in evacuation, roadblocks and other responses.

I would be remiss if I didn't pont out to everyone that many things were managed well during the incident Sunday. The County emergency directors' organization responded effectively; roadblocks were in place effectively; emergency treatment centers were quickly set up; and the hospital emergency rooms performed most admirably.

The good points not withstanding, Union Carbide intends to include as part of its investigation a critical review of this process, for it has implications for the entire chemical industry, not just Union Carbide.

##

0342T

**CONTACT:**

Ed Van Den Ameele
(203) 794-6985
   or
Harvey Cobert
(203) 794-7027
   or
Tom Failla
(203) 794-6928

RECEIVED

AUG 19 1985

T. D. EPPS

### REPORT ON INSTITUTE INCIDENT WILL BE MADE
### NEXT WEEK, SAYS UNION CARBIDE CHAIRMAN

CHARLESTON, WV, August 16 -- A Union Carbide report on the causes of the incident at the company's Institute, West Virginia plant will be made next week, Union Carbide Chairman Warren M. Anderson said today at a press briefing here. He emphasized that the company is also cooperating fully with the Occupational, Safety and Health Administration; Environmental Protection Agency, and state and county officials in their investigations.

While complimenting the cooperation and team work of community and plant people during the incident, Mr. Anderson said the company's response to emergencies is being evaluated. New plant procedures will be to err on the side of caution and early warning. "From now on," he said, "we will pull the cord first, then apologize if it wasn't necessary."

Mr. Anderson reported that company officials will be holding meetings with community leaders. "There has to be an understanding between the community and the company that we know what we're doing, that we can handle overselves under all circumstances, and that there is a willingness and a desire and a need to work together," he said.

- MORE -

1985
P-1-6-04-85-070

"The chemical industry has had a good track record here and the communities and companies have worked together effectively over a long period of time," said Mr. Anderson. "Carbiders are a part of this community. They live here, they work here, they associate with their friends and neighbors, and they're proud of what they do. I have every degree of confidence in their professionalism and their capabilities."

A separate and independent investigation of the incident is being conducted by the Union Carbide Board of Directors' health, safety and environmental affairs committee.

- END -

# APPENDIX G

## HYPOTHESES DEVELOPED DURING FOCUSED GROUP INTERVIEWS

1. **Respondents trust the chemical companies**

   A clear consensus of those interviewed had a favorable impression of the chemical companies and believed that the economic benefits of the industry far outweigh the environmental risks.

2. **People agree the Valley needs the chemical companies**

   Most respondents believe that the economy of the Kanawha Valley would "die" if the chemical companies left because they could no longer operate profitably.

3. **Communities feel protected against risk**

   Respondents felt reasonably protected from environmental risks because the federal government had forced companies to improve health and safety--even though they had strong concerns about EPA's ability to regulate effectively and fairly.

4. **Individuals don't feel personally at risk**

   Because people trust the chemical companies, depend on them for jobs, and feel protected by the government, they do not feel personally at risk from emissions or accidents.

5. **Everyone feels the national media distorts news about accidents**

   Most respondents believed that the media had blown such incidents as the August Union Carbide leak at Institute out of proportion and were angry at what they saw as bad publicity for the Valley.

6. **Communities want more say**

   Respondents said they want better communications between their communities and the chemical companies and want more say in governmental and company decisions which affect their communities.

7. **No one wants to increase environmental risks**

   Residents and activists both opposed relaxing environmental standards to create jobs.

8. **People will consider both economic and environmental trade-offs**

   Because people are concerned about both their jobs and their health, they are willing to make economic and environmental trade-offs.

9. **The activists' views**

   Even activists, who admitted difficulty talking about the economic benefits of the chemical industry, felt they had to discuss the economic costs of environmental improvements in order to have their arguments considered by other residents.